TO:

FROM:

DATE:

Printed in China
978-1-5359-1486-4

1 2 3 4 5 6 7 8 • 22 21 20 19 18

Instruct the wise, and he will be wiser still;
teach the righteous, and he will learn more.
~Proverbs 9:9~

Date: ______

Title: ______

Verse: ______

Speaker: ______

Notes

How I Can Apply This

Date:

Title:

Verse:

Speaker:

Notes

How I Can Apply This

Date:

Title:

Verse:

Speaker:

Notes

How I Can Apply This

Date: __________

Title: __________

Verse: __________

Speaker: __________

Notes

How I Can Apply This

Date: ____________

Title: ____________

Verse: ____________

Speaker: ____________

Notes

How I Can Apply This

Date: ____________

Title: ____

Verse: ____

Speaker: ____

Notes

How I Can Apply This

Date:

Title:

Verse:

Speaker:

Notes

How I Can Apply This

Date:

Title:

Verse:

Speaker:

Notes

How I Can Apply This

Date: ____________

Title: ____

Verse: ____

Speaker: ____

Notes

How I Can Apply This

Date: ______

Title: ______

Verse: ______

Speaker: ______

Notes

How I Can Apply This

Date:

Title:

Verse:

Speaker:

Notes

How I Can Apply This

Date:

Title:

Verse:

Speaker:

Notes

How I Can Apply This

Date:

Title:

Verse:

Speaker:

Notes

How I Can Apply This

Date: ____________

Title: ____________

Verse: ____________

Speaker: ____________

Notes

How I Can Apply This

Date: ____________

Title: ____

Verse: ____

Speaker: ____

Notes

How I Can Apply This

Date:

Title:

Verse:

Speaker:

Notes

How I Can Apply This

Date:

Title:

Verse:

Speaker:

Notes

How I Can Apply This

Date: __________

Title: __________

Verse: __________

Speaker: __________

Notes

How I Can Apply This

Date: ____________

Title: ____________

Verse: ____________

Speaker: ____________

Notes

How I Can Apply This

Date: ____________

Title: ____________

Verse: ____________

Speaker: ____________

Notes

How I Can Apply This

Date: ____________

Title: ____________

Verse: ____________

Speaker: ____________

Notes

How I Can Apply This

Date: ____________

Title: ____________

Verse: ____________

Speaker: ____________

Notes

How I Can Apply This

Date:

Title:

Verse:

Speaker:

Notes

How I Can Apply This

Date:

Title:

Verse:

Speaker:

Notes

How I Can Apply This

Date: ___________

Title: ___________

Verse: ___________

Speaker: ___________

Notes

How I Can Apply This

Date: ____________

Title: ____________

Verse: ____________

Speaker: ____________

Notes

How I Can Apply This

Date:

Title:

Verse:

Speaker:

Notes

How I Can Apply This

Date:

Title:

Verse:

Speaker:

Notes

How I Can Apply This

Date:

Title:

Verse:

Speaker:

Notes

How I Can Apply This

Date: ______________

Title: ____

Verse: ____

Speaker: ____

Notes

How I Can Apply This

Date: ____________

Title: ____________

Verse: ____________

Speaker: ____________

Notes

How I Can Apply This

Date: ______

Title: ______

Verse: ______

Speaker: ______

Notes

How I Can Apply This

Date:

Title:

Verse:

Speaker:

Notes

How I Can Apply This

Date: ______________

Title: ______________

Verse: ______________

Speaker: ______________

Notes

How I Can Apply This

Date: ____________

Title: ____________

Verse: ____________

Speaker: ____________

Notes

How I Can Apply This

Date:

Title:

Verse:

Speaker:

Notes

How I Can Apply This

Date: ______________

Title: ______________

Verse: ______________

Speaker: ______________

Notes

How I Can Apply This

Date:

Title:

Verse:

Speaker:

Notes

How I Can Apply This

Date:

Title:

Verse:

Speaker:

Notes

How I Can Apply This

Date: ____________

Title: ____________

Verse: ____________

Speaker: ____________

Notes

How I Can Apply This

Date: ____________

Title: ____________

Verse: ____________

Speaker: ____________

Notes

How I Can Apply This

Date:

Title:

Verse:

Speaker:

Notes

How I Can Apply This

Date: ____________

Title: ____________

Verse: ____________

Speaker: ____________

Notes

How I Can Apply This

Date:

Title:

Verse:

Speaker:

Notes

How I Can Apply This

Date:

Title:

Verse:

Speaker:

Notes

How I Can Apply This

Date: ___________

Title: ___________

Verse: ___________

Speaker: ___________

Notes

How I Can Apply This

Date: ____________

Title: ____________

Verse: ____________

Speaker: ____________

Notes

How I Can Apply This

Date: ____________

Title: ____

Verse: ____

Speaker: ____

Notes

How I Can Apply This

Date: ____________

Title: ____________

Verse: ____________

Speaker: ____________

Notes

How I Can Apply This

Date:

Title:

Verse:

Speaker:

Notes

How I Can Apply This

Date:

Title:

Verse:

Speaker:

Notes

How I Can Apply This

Date:

Title:

Verse:

Speaker:

Notes

How I Can Apply This

Date: ____________

Title: ______________________________

Verse: ______________________________

Speaker: ______________________________

Notes

How I Can Apply This

Date:

Title:

Verse:

Speaker:

Notes

How I Can Apply This

Date: ____________

Title: ____

Verse: ____

Speaker: ____

Notes

How I Can Apply This

Date:

Title:

Verse:

Speaker:

Notes

How I Can Apply This

Date:

Title:

Verse:

Speaker:

Notes

How I Can Apply This

Date:

Title:

Verse:

Speaker:

Notes

How I Can Apply This

Date:

Title:

Verse:

Speaker:

Notes

How I Can Apply This

Date: ____________

Title: ____________

Verse: ____________

Speaker: ____________

Notes

How I Can Apply This

Date: ______________

Title: ____

Verse: ____

Speaker: ____

Notes

How I Can Apply This

Date:

Title:

Verse:

Speaker:

Notes

How I Can Apply This